Colour and Mood

By Julie Haydon

T0342752

Contents

Different Colours

Different colours can create different moods. A mood is how someone is feeling at a certain time and in a certain place.

People often use different colours to create different moods when decorating their homes. Most rooms have one or two main colours.

Blue is the colour of the summer sea and sky. It is a cool, calming colour.

Blue has been used to create a relaxing mood in this bathroom. The blue walls and the blue tiles give the room a holiday feel.

Yellow is the colour of the Sun and daffodils. It is a warm, cheerful colour.

Yellow has been used to create a happy mood in this bedroom. The yellow walls match the yellow in the bedcover.

Red is the colour of tomatoes and poppies. It is a warm, exciting colour.

Red has been used to create a bright mood in this dining room. The red walls stimulate the appetite.

Green is the colour of grass and leaves in spring. It is a cool, restful colour.

Green has been used to create a calming mood in this home office. The green walls pick up the green of the trees in the garden outside.

White is the colour of snow and milk. It is a cool, peaceful colour.

White has been used to create a simple, clean look in this kitchen. The crisp white furniture and walls give the room a modern feel.

Changing the main colour of a room can change the mood it creates.

Choose Paint Colours Carefully

It is important to choose paint colours carefully when decorating your home. Colours help to set the mood.

The right colours should suit the style of your house as well as your furniture and personality.

First, think about the mood you want to create in each room. If you want people to feel relaxed in a particular room, then you may want to choose a cool colour like blue. To create a bright mood, you may want to choose a warm colour like red.

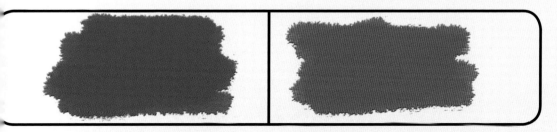

It is a good idea to think about the style of your house. Black and white can look good in modern homes. Bright colours suit modern homes too. Darker colours and natural colours often look good in older homes.

Also, the main colour you choose for a room should suit the colour and style of the furniture. A living room with modern, navy furniture may look good with cheerful yellow walls. A bedroom with an older style of bed and a pink and white bedcover may look good with soft pink walls.

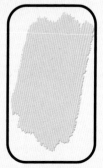

Finally, choose colours for your home that suit you. If you are a quiet person then choose a calming colour, like pale green.

If you are a bright, confident person, think about putting orange and purple together.

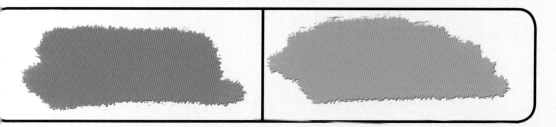

There are many paint colours for you to choose from. Take your time choosing the right colours for your home and you will create a home that suits you.